TOEFL Idioms

Flashcards

Other Kaplan Books for English Learners

TOEFL iBT with *CD-ROM*

TOEFL CBT Exam

Inside the TOEFL iBT

TOEFL Paper-and-Pencil

TOEFL Listening Practice

Kaplan TOEIC Exam, Second Edition

Learn English Through Classic Literature Series

The Short Stories and Essays of Mark Twain

American Tales of Horror and the Supernatural

TOEFL Idioms Flashcards

KAPLAN
PUBLISHING
New York • Chicago

Editorial Director: Jennifer Farthing
Senior Editor: Ruth Baygell
Project Editor: Katherine Martin
Production Editor: Mike Hankes
Production Artist: Virginia Byrne
Cover Designer: Carly Schnur

Published by Kaplan Publishing, a division of Kaplan, Inc.
888 Seventh Ave.
New York, NY 10106

Printed in the United States of America

October 2006
10 9 8 7 6 5 4 3 2 1

ISBN-13: 978-1-4195-9148-8
ISBN-10: 1-4195-9148-7

Kaplan Publishing books are available at special quantity discounts to use for sales promotions, employee premiums, or educational purposes. Please call our Special Sales Department to order or for more information at 800-621-9621, ext. 4444, e-mail kaplanpubsales@kaplan.com, or write to Kaplan Publishing, 30 South Wacker Drive, Suite 2500, Chicago, IL 60606-7481.

HOW TO USE THIS BOOK

The TOEFL (Test of English as a Foreign Language) is a standardized test designed to measure your ability to understand and use English as it is used in a North American university setting. Recent changes to the TOEFL have shifted the focus from how much you know about English to how well you comprehend, speak, and write English.

Whether you are taking TOEFL iBT, TOEFL CBT, or TOEFL Pencil-and-Paper, Kaplan's *TOEFL Idioms Flashcards* is perfectly designed to help you learn 350 idioms frequently used in English.

An idiom is a word or phrase that has a special meaning apart from its literal translation—it is usually a metaphor. Only people who are good at speaking English will know what an idiom means. Idioms can be difficult to learn, and they require time and patience to master well.

With this book, read the idiom on the front of the flashcard to determine whether you know it; on the reverse side, its definition and a sample sentence are offered to be sure that you understand its correct usage.

Once you have mastered a particular idiom, clip or fold back the corner of the flashcard so that you can skip over it to get to the words you still need to study.

The words are organized according to their part of speech. In some cases, two parts of speech are common, and we have noted these cases with more illustrative examples.

You will also see some notes in square brackets [ ]. This provides additional information about the origins of the idiom that should make it easier to memorize.

In some cases—mainly with verb phrases—some words are interchangeable. In such situations, we have provided two example sentences, one for each version. The most common version appears in the first sentence.

Study the idioms in any order and start on any page. Remember to flip the book over and study the other half.

Good luck!

spontaneously or impulsively; without prior planning

They were supposed to stay home this weekend, but, ***on the spur of the moment****, they decided to go camping instead.*

TO PUSH THE ENVELOPE

verb

ON THE SPUR OF THE MOMENT

adverb

to do something new and different that goes beyond what was previously thought to be possible; to innovate

*His new website really **pushes the envelope** of what the Internet can be used for.*

individually; in succession; one at a time

*When your work seems overwhelming, it can be helpful to deal with your assignments **one by one,** instead of trying to accomplish everything at once.*

Adjective

TO ABIDE BY THE RULES

verb

ONE BY ONE

adverb

to accept and follow (a law, ruling, etc.); to comply with

Both companies claim the right to sell the product, but they will ***abide by*** *the judge's decision.*

usually; in general

*I don't like documentary films **as a rule**, but this one is extremely interesting.*

TO CARRY ON DOING SOMETHING

verb

AS A RULE

adverb

to continue

The book was so interesting, he ***carried on*** *reading it after the end of study hall.*

They will ***carry on*** *with the dance lessons until they master the tango.*

actually; in fact

*The outcome of a military conflict is not simply based on casualties; **as a matter of fact**, the Union Army suffered greater losses than the Confederate Army in the American Civil War.*

TO TEST THE WATERS

verb

to check the likelihood of success before proceeding

Before announcing their new initiative, the politicians ***tested the waters*** *by conducting polls on the likely public response.*

AS A MATTER OF FACT

adverb

including a person's faults as well as his or her positive qualities

*Parents love their children unconditionally, **warts and all**.*

Adjective

TO PAN OUT

verb

WARTS AND ALL

adverb

to yield good results; to turn out well

He has had several job interviews, but nothing has ***panned out*** *yet.*

[from to *pan for gold*: to attempt to extract gold from a river] unanimously; in unison

*The company's employees opposed the policy **with one voice**.*

TO ACCOUNT FOR A DISCREPANCY

verb

WITH ONE VOICE

adverb

to explain; to be or provide an explanation for

The police asked him ***to account for*** *the missing money.*

The full moon ***accounts for*** *the exceptionally high tide today.*

1. immediately; 2. in an awkward position where one is forced to make a difficult decision right away

She didn't expect to get an answer for several weeks, but they accepted her application ***on the spot****.*

He put me ***on the spot*** *by proposing marriage in front of his whole family.*

TO GIVE AWAY THE ENDING

verb

ON THE SPOT

adverb

to reveal (information that was supposed to be kept secret)

The party was supposed to be a surprise, but my little sister ***gave it away.***

based on the appearance of something; apparently

From the looks of *the orientation assembly, there must be fewer students at school this year.*

The bake sale is raising a lot of money this year, ***by the looks of*** *it.*

TO FOLLOW SUIT

verb

FROM THE LOOKS OF

adverb

to do the same; to follow the example set by someone else

He decided to skip the tournament, and the rest of the team ***followed suit.***

[a reference to card games in which all players must play a card of the same suit as the one led by the first player] without using a machine

Delicate fabrics like cashmere should be washed ***by hand****.*

TO GROW OUT OF SOMETHING

verb

BY HAND

adverb

1. to become too large for (something); to outgrow; 2. to develop on the basis of (something)

*She gives her son's clothes to charity when he **grows out of** them.*

*This book **grew out of** a series of lectures I gave last year.*

despite it being very unlikely; incredibly, unexpectedly

***Against all odds**, she won her match against the five-time state champion.*

*He recovered from the operation and, **against all odds**, was able to walk again.*

TO BACK UP DATA

verb

AGAINST ALL ODDS

adverb

to make an electronic copy (of a computer file, etc.) as security in case the original is damaged or deleted

The power outage wasn't a problem because we ***had*** *already* ***backed up*** *the files on the computer.*

in addition; beyond what is needed

The recipe called for four cloves of garlic, but I added two more ***for good measure****.*

verb

TO KNOW THE ROPES

FOR GOOD MEASURE

adverb

to understand how things are done in a particular place

To succeed in a new job, ask someone who really ***knows the ropes*** *to train you.*

Hence ***to show someone the ropes*** means 'to show someone how things are done.'

[a reference to old-fashioned sailing ships, which had complicated ropes and riggings] considering; because of; taking into account

*She was given a lighter punishment **in light of** the fact that this was the first time she had broken the rules.*

TO BACK SOMEONE **INTO A CORNER**

verb

IN LIGHT OF

adverb

to put (someone or oneself) into a position where there is no way out and no room to maneuver

His political opponents tried to ***back*** *him* ***into a corner*** *so that any position he took would cause him to lose support.*

She ***has painted*** *herself* ***into a corner*** *by setting the standards so high that no one—including herself—can meet them.*

up to the present time; as of now

They will be hiring a new secretary, but, ***as yet****, they have not done so.*

TO HAVE SECOND THOUGHTS

verb

IT HAS NOT HAPPENED **AS YET.**

adverb

After I saw the reading list, I ***had second thoughts*** about taking the class.

to reconsider

in general; mostly

Her grades this year were good ***for the most part.***

TO LOOK AFTER A CHILD

verb

FOR THE MOST PART

adverb

to take care of

*She **looks after** her little brother after school every day.*

incidentally

I read that book you lent me. ***By the way****, did you know the author lives near here?*

Adverb

TO LOOK FORWARD TO AN EVENT

verb

BY THE WAY

adverb

to anticipate (something) with pleasure

I ***am looking forward to*** *the concert next week.*

after a long time; in the end; eventually

*It may seem hard to save money for retirement now, but, **in the long run**, you will be very glad that you did.*

Adverb

TO LOOK INTO SOMETHING

verb

IN THE LONG RUN

adverb

to investigate; to seek information about

*We **are looking into** buying a camper for our summer trip.*

considering; taking into account

*His writing is especially impressive **in view of** the fact that English is not his first language.*

TO KEEP ONE'S OPTIONS OPEN

verb

IN VIEW OF

adverb

to avoid doing anything that might rule out a future course of action

He will probably matriculate to State University, but he ***is keeping his options open*** *until he has gotten a response from all of the schools he applied to.*

back to the point where one started, as if no progress had been made

If this doesn't work, we can go ***back to square one****.*

Their first plan failed, so now they are ***back at square one****.*

TO BRING THE FACTS **HOME** TO HER

verb

BACK TO SQUARE ONE

adverb

to make (the reality of something) clear

This book finally ***brought*** *the complexity of the issue* ***home*** *to me.*

as ordinarily or habitually happens; like always

*I planned to study before class today, but, **as usual**, I overslept.*

Adverb

TO BRING NEW INFORMATION **TO LIGHT**

verb

YOU'RE LATE, **AS USUAL.**

adverb

to reveal; to uncover

*Their study **brought to light** some long-forgotten manuscripts.*

absolutely not; not at all

*She is a talented singer but **by no means** the best in the choir.*

See ***by all means***.

TO SEE THE LIGHT

verb

BY NO MEANS

adverb

to finally realize something after serious consideration

I thought he would never agree with me, but he eventually ***saw the light.***

certainly; definitely

If you go to that restaurant, ***by all means*** *try the salmon.*

See ***by no means***.

verb

TO LOOK UP

BY ALL MEANS

adverb

to show signs of improvement

She had more tests done, and the doctors say her health ***is looking up.***

for now; at this time, but not necessarily in the future

Let's keep this project a secret ***for the time being****.*

TO LOOK SOMETHING **UP**

verb

FOR THE TIME BEING

adverb

to seek information about (something) in a reference work

*I **looked up** the words I didn't know in a dictionary.*

because of; on the basis of

She got the job ***by virtue of*** *her superior language skills.*

TO LOOK UP TO SOMEONE

verb

BY VIRTUE OF

adverb

to have respect and admiration for (someone)

*He has always **looked up to** his uncle, who is a teacher.*

very quickly; right away

The cookies are almost done; they will be ready ***in no time****.*

TO GIVE SOMEONE **FREE REIN**

verb

IN NO TIME

adverb

to put few restrictions on the behavior of (someone)

*The new teacher **gives** the students **free rein** to study whatever they want.*

See *to rein* someone *in.*

[A *rein* is the strap used to control a horse while riding.]

in someone's opinion

I thought it was great, but ***as far as*** *he* ***was concerned****, it was the worst movie of the year.*

TO REIN SOMEONE **IN**

verb

AS FAR AS SOMEONE **IS CONCERNED**

adverb

to control (someone's) behavior closely

Whenever he began to stray from the task, our supervisor ***reined*** *him* ***in.***

See *to give someone free rein.*

according to the rules or directions; correctly

There weren't any violations—she did everything ***by the book****.*

TO GIVE HER STORY **THE BENEFIT OF THE DOUBT**

verb

BY THE BOOK

adverb

to assume that (a person or statement) is truthful until proven otherwise

His alibi is suspicious, but let's ***give*** *him* ***the benefit of the doubt*** *until we know more.*

in a situation for which one is not qualified or prepared

*He got **in over his head** when he agreed to do all of the paperwork for the project.*

TO HOLD ONE'S OWN

verb

IN OVER ONE'S HEAD

adverb

to perform reasonably well in a challenging situation

*The other runners in the race are much more experienced, but he **is holding his own** and will probably finish right in the middle.*

at stake; at risk

*Applying to college is very stressful; sometimes it feels like your entire future is **in the balance**.*

TO HOLD ONE'S TONGUE

verb

IN THE BALANCE

adverb

Adjective

to stay silent; to refrain from speaking

*She was upset and wanted to say something, but she **held her tongue.***

without any doubt at all; for certain

We now know ***beyond a shadow of a doubt*** *that the Vikings reached North America centuries before Columbus.*

TO BRING SOMETHING **TO MIND**

verb

BEYOND THE SHADOW OF A DOUBT

adverb

to be reminiscent of (something); to remind

*This dish **brings to mind** a meal I once had in Paris.*

without any warning; instantly

*We were walking in the park when **all of the sudden** the lights went out.*

TO SET THE RECORD STRAIGHT

verb

ALL OF A SUDDEN

adverb

to correct a false story; to provide accurate information

The media initially reported that the escaped animal was a tiger, but zoo officials ***set the record straight****, announcing that it was a harmless kangaroo.*

out of public view

> *The agreement between the two leaders seemed spontaneous, but a lot of negotiations were conducted* ***behind the scenes*** *to make it happen.*

[a reference to theaters, where preparations take place *behind the scenery*, out of sight of the audience]

TO **USE UP** A RESOURCE

verb

BEHIND THE SCENES

adverb

to consume (something) completely

I couldn't brush my teeth this morning because my brother ***had used up*** *the toothpaste.*

when someone is not around

It is unfair to criticize him ***behind*** *his* ***back*** *when he can't defend himself.*

You shouldn't say anything ***behind*** *her* ***back*** *that you wouldn't say to her face.*

TO SIZE UP THE COMPETITION

verb

BEHIND SOMEONE'S **BACK**

adverb

to evaluate or assess

The dogs growled and walked in a circle, ***sizing*** *each other* ***up.***

through informal conversation

> *They didn't have enough money to advertise in the newspaper, but they got a lot of publicity* ***by word of mouth****.*

Also as an adjective: ***word-of-mouth*** *advertising.*

Noun

TO HAVE ONE'S HANDS TIED

verb

BY WORD OF MOUTH

adverb

Idiom

to be restricted; to be prevented from doing something

*I wish I could give you more information, but **my hands are tied.***

*The government was unable to respond quickly because **its hands were tied** by regulations.*

excessively; so much that it causes problems

*She is careful **to a fault**; it takes her forever to finish anything.*

TO LOWER THE BAR

verb

TO A FAULT

adverb

Idiom

to reduce standards so that it is easier to succeed

When no one qualified under the original criteria, the admissions committee ***lowered the bar.***

in the future; eventually

This may seem like a good policy now, but it could cause major problems ***down the line****.*

Noun

TO FLARE UP

verb

DOWN THE LINE

adverb

Idiom

to erupt or break out; to recur

*My doctor had said the rash on my knee was cured, but it **flared up** again.*

in a short summary; very briefly

This book covers the major points of the topic ***in a nutshell****.*

TO ASK AFTER SOMEONE

verb

IN A NUTSHELL

adverb

Idiom

to inquire about the well-being of (someone)

*He heard your mother was in the hospital and called **to ask after** her.*

with interruptions; intermittently

*It rained **on and off** all night but never for very long.*

TO HOLD SWAY

verb

ON AND OFF

adverb

to dominate; to have great influence

*The Dutch **held sway** in New York until 1664, when the English took control.*

personally; directly; in person

I had heard that the Grand Canyon was impressive, but I didn't appreciate its enormity until I saw it ***at first hand****.*

TO GO THROUGH WITH

verb

WE EXPERIENCED IT **AT FIRST HAND**

adverb

Idiom

to perform (an action) as planned; to carry out

*We **went through with** our plan to have a picnic despite the rain.*

without proper permission or disclosure; illegally

*He was getting paid **under the table** to avoid taxes.*

See ***above board***

TO END UP

verb

UNDER THE TABLE

adverb

Idiom

to come eventually to a particular situation or place

*It **ended up** costing much more than we expected.*

*After walking for hours, they **ended up** in the same place where they started.*

nevertheless

Some say that printed books are becoming obsolete; ***be that as it may****, publishing remains a dynamic and prosperous business.*

TO LAY CLAIM TO PROPERTY

verb

BE THAT AS IT MAY

adverb

to assert that one has the right to (something); to claim ownership of

*My sister always **laid claim to** the top bunk bed, so I was stuck on the bottom.*

as a representative of someone; in the interest of someone

*He wrote a letter **on behalf of** his mother, asking the company to give her a refund.*

TO CROSS ONE'S MIND

verb

ON BEHALF OF SOMEONE

adverb

to occur to one

I'm so accustomed to flying that the possibility of driving home never ***crossed my mind.***

in secret; out of public view

The government eventually signed the treaty, but we may never know what bargains were made ***behind closed doors*** *to make it happen.*

TO HOLD ON TO SHARES IN THE COMPANY

verb

BEHIND CLOSED DOORS

adverb

---

to keep or retain

He considered selling his motorcycle, but he decided ***to hold on to*** *it.*

in one's thoughts; preoccupying one

*I have a lot **on my mind** right now.*

*That incident has been **on his mind** lately.*

Pronoun

TO HOLD OUT

verb

ON ONE'S MIND

adverb

to resist or endure in a challenging situation

Her doctor advised her to give up meat, and she ***held out*** *for six months before giving in to temptation.*

based on the information (a person) has; to the best of (a person's) knowledge

*She isn't here yet, but **as far as I know** she is still planning to come.*

TO LEAVE NO STONE UNTURNED

verb

AS FAR AS HE KNOWS

adverb

to look everywhere; to attempt everything

*We **left no stone unturned** in our search for the city's best hot dog.*

without any warning; unexpectedly; out of nowhere

*I hadn't seen him in months, but he called me **out of the blue** last week and invited me to dinner.*

Pronoun

TO CROSS PATHS

verb

OUT OF THE BLUE

adverb

to meet by chance

They ***crossed paths*** *in Italy when they both happened to be vacationing there.*

He ***crossed paths*** *with my sister in college.*

in addition to; besides

On top of *all of his other accomplishments, he is now captain of the hockey team.*

TO RUN INTO SOMEONE

verb

ON TOP OF EVERYTHING ELSE

adverb

Verb

to meet (someone) by chance

*I hadn't seen him in months, but I **ran into** him at the supermarket last week.*

certainly; absolutely; unquestionably

*It was **without a doubt** the worst book I have ever read.*

Pronoun

TO HAVE ONE'S WORK CUT OUT FOR ONE

verb

WITHOUT A DOUBT

adverb

Verb

to have a lot of work to do in order to accomplish something

If she wants to finish this drawing before the art fair, ***she has her work cut out for her.***

worth mentioning

*He doesn't have any savings **to speak of**; he spends all of his money on entertainment.*

TO GET ONE'S ACT TOGETHER

verb

NO ACCOMPLISHMENTS **TO SPEAK OF**

adverb

to prepare oneself to accomplish something; to get organized

*We need **to get our act together** if we're going to finish this by Friday.*

through good times and bad times; in all circumstances

*Married couples vow to support each other **through thick and thin**.*

TO DROP BY

verb

THROUGH THICK AND THIN

adverb

to make a short, usually unannounced, visit

He ***dropped by*** *for a few minutes last night.*

as a consequence of; in the aftermath of

In the wake of *the recent earthquake, we decided to redesign the building for stability.*

TO DROP IN ON SOMEONE

verb

IN THE WAKE OF

adverb

*On the way home, we **dropped in on** my grandmother to see how she was doing.*

to make a short, usually unannounced, visit to (a person)

at risk; in question

*The national championship is **at stake** in this game.*

TO HAVE ONE'S HANDS FULL

verb

AT STAKE

adverb

to be very busy; to have a lot to do

*She has **had her hands full** lately, so she probably won't be able to help you.*

in advance; beforehand

He practiced an acceptance speech ***ahead of time*** *just in case he won the prize.*

TO GO WRONG

verb

PREPARED **AHEAD OF TIME**

adverb

Verb

to cause a failure; to go amiss

The experiment failed, but scientists still are not sure what ***went wrong.***

in the future

This may seem like a risky investment now, but I am confident that it will pay ***down the road****.*

TO ERR ON THE SIDE OF CAUTION

verb

DOWN THE ROAD

adverb

to emphasize (a particular aspect of an issue) so that if a mistake is made, it will enhance that aspect

No one knows what level of pollutants is safe for fish, so it seems best ***to err on the side of*** *conservation by stopping all pollution in the river.*

without important information; uninformed

*She was upset that they had kept her **in the dark** about their plan to sell the house.*

TO REST ON ONE'S LAURELS

verb

HE WAS LEFT **IN THE DARK**

adverb

to be satisfied with one's past accomplishments rather than attempting anything new

Since his highly praised first novel came out, he ***has been resting on his laurels*** *and hasn't written anything new.*

[a reference to the ancient Greek tradition of crowning a person with a wreath of *laurels*, or bay leaves, to honor a great accomplishment]

1. while holding hands; 2. in close association; jointly

Couples walked down the street ***hand in hand****.*

Low unemployment often goes ***hand in hand*** *with inflation.*

TO TAKE ONE'S TIME

verb

HAND IN HAND

adverb

to proceed slowly; to avoid rushing

I am taking my time on this paper, since it isn't due until the end of the semester.

occasionally

*He doesn't exercise much, but he does go biking **now and then**.*

TO TIGHTEN ONE'S BELT

verb

NOW AND THEN

adverb

to take extreme measures in order to economize; to cut back

Our funding has been cut, so we are going to have ***to tighten our belts*** *and reduce the budget.*

[a reference to losing weight from eating less, which might cause someone to need a smaller belt] without any preparation

*Everyone was impressed when he gave a fantastic speech **off the cuff**.*

TO TOUCH ON A SUBJECT

verb

SPEAKING **OFF THE CUFF**

adverb

Pronoun

to address (a topic) briefly

*The course will mainly cover the works of Jean-Jacques Rousseau, but it will also **touch on** some of his contemporaries, such as Voltaire and Diderot.*

in contradiction to; in disagreement or conflicting with

His account of events is ***at odds with*** *the story published in the newspaper.*

TO SEE EYE TO EYE

verb

AT ODDS WITH ESTABLISHED THEORY

adverb

to have similar opinions; to understand each other

They have almost nothing in common, but when it comes to baseball, they ***see eye to eye.***

for all; in every category

The new budget makes cutbacks in government services ***across the board****, from highways to education.*

TO HAVE A SAY

verb

ACROSS THE BOARD

adverb

to have a degree of influence or power

*It is important for children **to have a say** in decisions about their activities.*

*In a democracy, citizens **have a voice** in their government.*

the most important consideration or conclusion; the main point

> *We talked about a lot of techniques for time management, but* ***the bottom line*** *is that we just need to get more done.*

[from the use of *the bottom line* in accounting, where it refers to the final total of a balance sheet]

TO CHERRY-PICK

verb

to take only the most desirable items available from among a selection

*She sells the most cars because she **cherry-picks** the most promising customers, leaving the rest of us with the reluctant ones.*

THE BOTTOM LINE

noun

a change from what is usual or ordinary

She usually drinks coffee every morning, but today she's having tea for ***a change of pace****.*

TO DO SOMEONE **GOOD**

verb

A CHANGE OF PACE

noun

to have a beneficial effect on (someone)

He has seemed very stressed out lately; a vacation will ***do*** *him* ***good****.*

a place that is insulated from the concerns of the real world

To really understand social issues, he needs to get away from the ***ivory tower*** *of university life.*

TO NARROW DOWN A LIST

verb

idiom

IVORY TOWER

noun

to reduce the number of options in (a selection)

*They started with a pool of twenty applicants, but they **narrowed** it **down** to three finalists.*

a victory that comes at too high a cost, leaving the winner worse off

*Nuclear deterrence is based on the fact that even for the winner, a nuclear war would result in a **Pyrrhic victory**.*

[a reference to an incident in ancient history (279 BC), when the army of King *Pyrrhus* of Epirus experienced such huge losses in defeating the Romans that he declared: 'One more such victory and I shall be lost']

Idiom

TO DRAW A BLANK

verb

PYRRHIC VICTORY

noun

to be unable to remember or respond

*I studied thoroughly for the test, but when I saw the first question, I just **drew a blank.***

a victory that accomplishes or signifies nothing

He won the race, but since all of the best competitors had dropped out, it was a ***hollow victory****.*

Idiom

TO DO ONE'S BEST

verb

to try as hard as possible

He didn't get a perfect score, but he ***did his best****, and that is what really matters.*

HOLLOW VICTORY

noun

a plan or set of circumstances that is doomed to produce terrible results

*Assigning the two of them to work on a project together is a **recipe for disaster**.*

Idiom

TO THROW DOWN THE GAUNTLET

verb

to issue a challenge

*The American colonists **threw down the gauntlet** to England in 1776 with the Declaration of Independence.*

[A *gauntlet* is a type of armored glove, which would traditionally be thrown down by a medieval knight in a challenge to an opponent. To accept the challenge, the opponent would pick up the glove; hence, to *take up the gauntlet* means 'to accept a challenge.']

RECIPE FOR DISASTER

noun

the latest, most up-to-date technology

Her new stereo is ***the state of the art*** *in audio equipment.*

Also as an adjective: ***state-of-the-art*** *technology*.

Idiom

TO THROW IN THE TOWEL

verb

THE STATE OF THE ART

noun

to accept defeat; to surrender

After struggling for many years with our business, we finally ***threw in the towel*** *after realizing we needed to make major renovations.*

a sudden and significant improvement or advance

> *In the past decade, there has been a* ***quantum leap*** *in our scientific understanding of human genetics.*

[from Physics, where a *quantum leap* (also ***quantum jump***) is the abrupt shift of an electron within an atom from one energy state to another]

TO THROW SOMEONE **TO THE WOLVES**

verb

QUANTUM LEAP

noun

to leave (someone) to face criticism or challenges alone; to abandon (someone)

He claimed not to know anything about the scandal and ***threw*** *his assistant* ***to the wolves*** profits or benefits acquired unfairly or illegally

*Robin Hood is both a thief and a hero because he shares his **ill-gotten gains** with the poor.*

---

idiom

TO FILL SOMEONE **IN**

verb

ILL-GOTTEN GAINS

noun

to inform (someone) fully; to give (someone) the details

Lisa missed the meeting where that was discussed, so someone will have ***to fill*** *her* ***in.***

the broad perspective on an issue; the overview

*The proposal should focus on **the big picture**; we don't want to get bogged down in the details.*

idiom

TO FILL IN FOR SOMEONE

verb

SEEING **THE BIG PICTURE**

noun

to replace or substitute for

I usually work on Mondays and Fridays, but I ***am filling in for*** *Mark today.*

a gesture of peace

After a hard-fought campaign, the winning politician offered his opponents an ***olive branch*** *by inviting them to join his cabinet.*

TO TAKE SOMEONE'S **PLACE**

verb

OLIVE BRANCH

noun

to replace or substitute for (someone)

*The star of the play got sick, so the understudy **took** her **place**.*

a project undertaken purely out of pleasure or interest

*He paints portraits for money, but his still-life paintings are a **labor of love**.*

idiom

TO COME TO GRIPS WITH A CHALLENGING CONCEPT

verb

A **LABOR OF LOVE**

noun

to become capable of dealing with or understanding

Many companies still haven't ***come to grips with*** *the new regulations.*

It took us a long time to ***get to grips with*** *this computer program.*

the days of one's youth, regarded either as a time of inexperience or as a peak or heyday

We recalled the rash decisions of our ***salad days****.*

His performance has declined since his ***salad days****.*

[from Shakespeare's A*nthony and Cleopatra*: my salad days, when I was green in judgment]

TO STAY OUT OF A DISPUTE

verb

SALAD DAYS

noun

to avoid getting involved in

*The United States **stayed out of** the First World War until April of 1917.*

attractive but unnecessary extra features

*For a little bit more money you can get the deluxe version of the car with all the **bells and whistles**.*

TO WEAR THIN

verb

BELLS AND WHISTLES

noun

to become less effective due to overuse

*You claim to have forgotten your homework at least once a week, so that excuse **is wearing thin.***

a person's real or authentic character

He seems very calm and polite, but his angry outburst yesterday revealed his ***true colors****.*

Adjective

TO SPEAK OUT ON A CONTROVERSIAL ISSUE

verb

TRUE COLORS

noun

to express one's opinions openly

It was nice to hear a politician ***speak out*** *about the problems facing farmers today.*

negative feelings of resentment or bitterness

*They are no longer in business together, but they are still friends, and there are no **hard feelings** about the end of their partnership.*

TO THINK UP A NEW GAME

verb

HARD FEELINGS

noun

to invent; to make up

Our math teacher ***is*** *always* ***thinking up*** *new ways to make sure we do our homework.*

a general or approximate guideline

*When cooking rice, a good **rule of thumb** is to use two parts water to one part rice.*

Adjective

TO TAKE ADVANTAGE OF SOMEONE OR SOMETHING

verb

RULE OF THUMB

noun

1. to exploit (someone); 2. to utilize or avail oneself of (something)

*They **were** only **taking advantage of** him and had no interest in really being his friends.*

*She is trying **to take advantage of** the many cultural experiences the city has to offer.*

a new or unfamiliar situation

Advances in biotechnology are taking scientists into ***uncharted waters*** *requiring new ethical guide-lines.*

[*uncharted* means ‘unmapped or unexplored’]

TO CARRY OUT ORDERS

verb

UNCHARTED WATERS

noun

to obey; to put into action

*He **carried out** your instructions perfectly; everything is the way you wanted it.*

an unpleasant fact that is difficult to accept

*The knee injury that ended his tennis career was a **bitter pill**, but he became a successful coach.*

TO MEET SOMEONE **HALFWAY**

verb

BITTER PILL

noun

to compromise with (someone)

We made several good offers, but he stubbornly stuck to his original price and refused ***to meet*** *us* ***halfway.***

the last possible moment

They waited until the ***eleventh hour*** *to make plans for their trip and had trouble getting a hotel room.*

Also as an adjective: *an* ***eleventh-hour*** *effort to conclude the talks.*

TO MEET ONE'S MATCH

verb

THE **ELEVENTH HOUR**

noun

to find one's equal

He is a great chess player, but in you he finally ***met his match.***

a cycle of negative effects that build off of one another, resulting in a worsening situation; a downward spiral

> *Some overweight children get caught in a* ***vicious circle****: they don't excel at athletics, so they get less exercise, which in turn makes them even more overweight.*

Also ***vicious cycle***.

TO KEEP A LOW PROFILE

verb

A **VICIOUS CIRCLE**

noun

to avoid getting attention or publicity

Like many celebrities, she started ***keeping a low profile*** *after she had children.*

the qualities required to accomplish something

*Your daughter has **what it takes** to be a professional musician.*

TO GET A MESSAGE **ACROSS**

verb

to express

*The president's latest speech really **got across** his concern about the need for more educational funding.*

noun

WHAT IT TAKES

a complete reversal; a U-turn

*After 10 years of supporting the same party, he did an **about face** and started voting for the opposition.*

TO GET AWAY WITH A CRIME

verb

ABOUT FACE

noun

to manage to escape the consequences of (an action)

I can't believe he ***got away with*** *cheating on that quiz.*

1. the value printed on a ticket, note of currency, etc.; 2. the apparent or superficial meaning of something

*We paid more than **face value** for the concert tickets.*

*If you take his last speech at **face value**, it sounds like he is planning radical changes.*

verb

TO THINK ON ONE'S FEET

FACE VALUE

noun

to react quickly and effectively without prior preparation

*She had **to think on her feet** when she was unexpectedly asked to lead the discussion.*

an issue about which there is no clear answer or where conventional standards don't seem to apply

> *A lot of Internet businesses operate in a* ***gray area****, and no one is sure what laws should apply to them.*

[from the idea that some issues are *neither black nor white*]

TO WASH ONE'S HANDS OF THE WHOLE AFFAIR

verb

to claim to no longer be responsible for or involved with (something); to dissociate oneself from

*He **has washed his hands of** the group since it participated in a controversial protest last year.*

noun

GRAY AREA

a fresh start, with any previous mistakes forgiven or forgotten

*He moved to a new school, where he could start over with **a clean slate**.*

TO SETTLE FOR A LOWER PRICE

verb

A CLEAN SLATE

noun

to accept less than desired or expected

*He had dreamed of becoming president, but he **settled for** being mayor of a small town.*

the one weak spot of an otherwise strong person

> *Although I am generally good in English, his first question found my* ***Achilles heel****: my ignorance of spelling rules.*

[in reference to the character *Achilles* in Greek mythology, who could only be injured on his heel]

TO CAST DOUBT ON SOMETHING

verb

HIS **ACHILLES HEEL**

noun

to make (something) appear doubtful or dubious

*The photos from the party **cast doubt on** his version of events.*

the forefront of progress within a field

*This scientist is doing work on **the cutting edge** of physics research.*

Also used as an adjective: ***cutting-edge** technology*.

TO MAKE A POINT OF DOING SOMETHING

verb

THE CUTTING EDGE

noun

to make a deliberate effort to do something

*I **make a point** of calling my grandmother once a week.*

a strategy

*What is your **game plan** for increasing profits?*

TO MAKE DO

verb

to manage without something important; to get by

*During the Second World War, cooks often **made do** without rationed ingredients like chocolate and sugar.*

noun

GAME PLAN

hostility caused by past events; ill will; antagonism; hatred

*There has been **bad blood** between them ever since the lawsuit 10 years ago.*

TO MAKE SURE

verb

BAD BLOOD

noun

to be certain; to confirm

*Before leaving the house, he **made sure** he had his keys.*

the better position in a situation; the advantage

*When the other team's best player was injured, we gained **the upper hand**.*

TO MAKE SENSE

verb

THE UPPER HAND

noun

to be reasonable or logical

Her theory ***makes sense.***

in excellent condition, as if new

*These antique toys are very valuable because they are still in **mint condition**.*

Also as an adjective: *a **mint-condition** car.*

[in reference to *mint*, a place where coins are made]

TO KEEP AN EYE ON SOMETHING

verb

MINT CONDITION

noun

to watch; to monitor

*Could you please **keep an eye on** the cake in the oven to make sure it doesn't burn?*

a policy of punishing even minor offenses

The school has instituted a policy of ***zero tolerance*** *for dress-code violations; last week, a student got detention for forgetting to wear a tie.*

Also as an adjective: a ***zero-tolerance*** *approach to law enforcement.*

TO **GET OVER** A SETBACK

verb

ZERO TOLERANCE

noun

to recover from; to bounce back from

*She **is** finally **getting over** her cold.*

*The team needs **to get over** today's loss and start preparing for the next game.*

a controversial issue that is an obstacle to making an agreement

They are close to signing a contract, but the number of vacation days is still a ***sticking point****.*

TO TAKE SOMEONE'S **WORD FOR IT**

verb

STICKING POINT

noun

to believe someone without additional evidence

*He says that he didn't take the money, and I **am taking** his **word for it.***

something that has the potential both to help and to hurt

*His talent is **a double-edged sword**: it brings him success but has also limited his options.*

Adverb

TO TAKE A BREAK

verb

DOUBLE-EDGED SWORD

noun

to take a rest; to stop an activity temporarily

She painted for hours at a time without ***taking a break.***

no extra time, meaning it is necessary to do something right away

*There is **no time to lose**, so let's get to work.*

TO DRAW THE LINE

verb

NO TIME TO LOSE

noun

to set a limit about how far one is willing to go

She is an adventurous eater, but she ***draws the line*** *at insects.*

I'll help you out one more time, but that is where I ***draw the line.***

a small but easily recognized part of a much larger problem or issue

*The corruption scandals reported in the news are only the **tip of the iceberg**.*

[a reference to the fact that the biggest part of an iceberg is hidden underneath the water—only the *tip* is visible]

TO THINK BETTER OF A DECISION

verb

THE TIP OF THE ICEBERG

noun

to decide against (doing something) after thinking about it more; to reconsider

*He had planned to take part in the prank, but he **thought better of** it and stayed home.*

polite conversation on unimportant topics; chat

*He made **small talk** with all of the guests at the party.*

TO THINK SOMETHING **OVER**

verb

SMALL TALK

noun

to consider (something) carefully

*I probably won't accept the job offer, but I **am** still **thinking it over**.*

excessive regulations and bureaucracy

We had to deal with a lot of ***red tape*** *to get the proper visa to travel here.*

[from the *reddish-colored tape* or ribbon that was once used to tie together bundles of legal documents]

TO THINK TWICE

verb

RED TAPE

noun

to consider carefully before making a decision

If I were you, I would ***think twice*** *about buying a used car over the Internet.*

When he was invited to give a speech at his old high school, he didn't ***think twice*** *before agreeing.*

an option which is bad, but still better than the alternative

I wasn't impressed with either of the candidates, but I voted for ***the lesser of two evils****.*

TO GET RID OF SOMETHING

verb

THE LESSER OF TWO EVILS

noun

to discard or eliminate

*We **got rid of** all the food in the refrigerator that was past its expiration date.*

journalism that is sensationalist and biased

That newspaper will print anything to sell papers—it's all gossip and ***yellow journalism****.*

Also ***yellow press***.

TO GET THE BEST OF SOMEONE

verb

Adjective

YELLOW JOURNALISM

noun

to defeat or outwit

He tried to stay awake for the fireworks at midnight, but his fatigue ***got the best of*** *him, and he fell asleep before 11:00.*

a person who is decent, honest, kind, and unpretentious

*Her parents are very nice people; they are the **salt of the earth**.*

Often used as an adjective: ***salt-of-the-earth** people*.

TO GET TO THE BOTTOM OF A MYSTERY

verb

SALT OF THE EARTH

noun

to uncover the truth about

We reported the strange sounds coming from the house next door, and the police promised ***to get to the bottom of*** *it.*

a lie considered to be harmless, often told out of politeness

*I told her she looked nice, but it was a **white lie**; her dress was too short.*

TO GET UNDERWAY

verb

to begin; to start

The annual Autumn Festival ***gets underway*** *next week.*

WHITE LIE

noun

the last of a series of problems or annoyances, which causes someone to finally give up

*We have put up with a leaky roof, dripping faucet, and heating problems in this apartment, but the roaches were **the last straw**; we are going to move out tomorrow.*

TO MINCE WORDS

verb

THE LAST STRAW

noun

to avoid directly saying something that might upset or offend; to euphemize

Tell me what you really thought of my performance, and don't ***mince words.***

the final option remaining when everything else has failed

*Doctors consider surgery for weight loss the **last resort** and only recommend it for people who are not helped by diet, exercise, or medication.*

TO JUMP ON THE BANDWAGON

verb

Idiom

AS A **LAST RESORT**

noun

to take up an activity or idea that is suddenly very popular

The price of the stock rose quickly as investors ***jumped on the bandwagon*** *and bought shares.*

She has listened to their music for years, but now everyone ***is getting on the bandwagon.***

the latest possible time

She always leaves her homework until ***the last minute****.*

Also as an adjective: ***last-minute*** *Christmas shopping*.

TO MAKE GOOD ON A PROMISE

verb

THE LAST MINUTE

noun

to follow through on

*The company **made good on** its pledge to donate new computers to the school.*

a new burst of energy or strength to continue a difficult effort

In the last week before the play opened, the actors got their ***second wind*** *and rehearsed long hours to ensure that it was a success.*

[originally used to describe the sudden ability to breathe more easily, which some people feel after exercising for a long time]

TO MAKE OFF WITH THE MONEY

verb

SECOND WIND

noun

Idiom

to take or steal (something); to abscond with

He was caught trying ***to make off with*** *two silver vases after the party.*

a person who is currently in a position of authority whose successor has already been chosen

*When a sitting president loses the election for a second term in November, he becomes a **lame duck** until the new president is inaugurated the following January.*

*Now that our company's CEO is a **lame duck**, people doubt that she will be able to accomplish much before she retires.*

TO STAND FOR

verb

LAME DUCK

noun

1. to support or advocate (a belief or principle); 2. to be an abbreviation of

*The memorial should express the ideals he **stood for** all his life: freedom and equality.*

*FBI **stands for** Federal Bureau of Investigation.*

a possession that is useless or unwanted and difficult to get rid of

*The paining is valuable, but no one wants a picture of a slaughterhouse, so it's really a **white elephant**.*

TO STAND UP FOR SOMEONE

verb

WHITE ELEPHANT

noun

Idiom

to defend; to advocate for

*She always **stood up for** her little brother when other children teased him.*

hope that a time of difficulty will end

He struggled to get out of debt for years, but he finally sees ***the light at the end of the tunnel****.*

TO STAND OUT

verb

THE LIGHT AT THE END OF THE TUNNEL

noun

Idiom

to be conspicuous; to attract attention

*The white flowers **stand out** against the dark background of the painting.*

the people who have authority

No changes can be made without approval from ***the powers that be****.*

TO WIND DOWN

verb

THE POWERS THAT BE

noun

1. to slow down; to draw to a close; 2. to relax (said of a person)

The wedding season hits its peak in June and starts ***to wind down*** *in September.*

After three days of tough hiking, we spent a day ***winding down*** *at the beach.*

positive and negative feelings felt at the same time

*She has **mixed emotions** about moving away; she's excited about the new house but worried about going to a new school.*

TO WIND UP SOMEWHERE

verb

MIXED EMOTIONS

noun

to find oneself in a place or situation; to arrive or end up

*I was as surprised as anyone when I **wound up** in the television industry.*

fairness; equality

Public schools are intended to create a ***level playing field*** *in education.*

TO KEEP AT A TASK

verb

LEVEL PLAYING FIELD

noun

Idiom

to continue to do; to persist or persevere with

*She had trouble at first, but she **kept at** it and is now one of the best gymnasts in the state.*

an assortment of random things

*His desk was covered with **odds and ends**, and it was impossible to find anything.*

TO KEEP INFORMATION **FROM** SOMEONE

verb

ODDS AND ENDS

noun

Idiom

to hide (something) from someone; to keep (something) secret from someone

Romeo and Juliet ***kept*** *their marriage* ***from*** *their families.*

an obvious outcome; a result that can be predicted in advance

Because of the home team's superior defense, it was a ***foregone conclusion*** *that they would win.*

TO KEEP FROM DOING SOMETHING

verb

to stop oneself from doing something; to refrain from or avoid

*When she saw his new haircut, she could hardly **keep from** laughing.*

FOREGONE CONCLUSION

noun

minor adjustments needed to perfect something

The car is running now, but we have to do some ***fine tuning*** *to make it ready to drive on the road.*

Also as a verb: *We need to* ***fine-tune*** *our performance.*

TO KEEP UP WITH SOMEONE OR SOMETHING

verb

1. to travel at the same speed as; to stay abreast of; 2. to stay informed about

*He couldn't **keep up with** the other cyclists on the hilly part of the course.*

*I try **to keep up with** the latest advances in computer science.*

noun

FINE TUNING

based on the efforts of ordinary people

*Our new city councilwoman didn't get a lot of support from powerful politicians, but she had a strong **grass-roots** campaign.*

Also as a noun: *support from the **grass roots**.*

Pronoun

TO LEND A HAND

verb

A **GRASS-ROOTS** EFFORT

adjective

to help

*Local charities **lent a hand** to the effort to rebuild after the earthquake.*

*Could you please **give me a hand** with this heavy box?*

unmanageable; out of control

*The absenteeism in this class is getting **out of hand**.*

TO JUMP TO CONCLUSIONS

verb

OUT OF HAND

adjective

to form an opinion about something quickly without examining all of the facts

A good doctor looks at all of a patient's symptoms carefully before making a diagnosis rather than just ***jumping to conclusions.***

far ahead; far more advanced

*Their science laboratories are **light years ahead** of the facilities at our university.*

TO SIT AROUND

verb

LIGHT YEARS AHEAD

adjective

to lounge or be idle; to hang around

He used to exercise a lot, but now he just ***sits around*** *playing video games.*

extremely sensitive; easily upset

*When students are too **thin-skinned**, it can be difficult to give them feedback on their work.*

The opposite is ***thick-skinned***.

TO SIT THROUGH A LONG CEREMONY

verb

THIN-SKINNED

adjective

to stay to the end of (an event or performance)

*I wanted to leave the play at intermission, but my parents made me **sit through** all three hours of it.*

showing signs of age or use

*This sofa was beautiful when it was new, but it is getting a bit **worse for wear**.*

TO SIT TIGHT

verb

WORSE FOR WEAR

adjective

to wait patiently

*Could you just **sit tight** for a little bit longer? I'm almost ready to leave.*

impossible; inconceivable; not worth considering

*Because of the recent snowstorm, driving over the mountain was **out of the question**.*

TO GET ON WITH AN ACTIVITY

verb

OUT OF THE QUESTION

adjective

to continue

We need to stop wasting time and ***get on with*** *studying for the exam.*

not talkative; reticent

My grandmother is a woman ***of few words****, but when she says something, it is usually very insightful.*

TO TAKE A PIECE OF INFORMATION **INTO ACCOUNT**

verb

A MAN **OF FEW WORDS**

adjective

to consider; to give attention to

The theory was flawed because it didn't ***take into account*** *the importance of environmental factors.*

up for discussion; possible as an option

We haven't made a final decision yet, so all of the proposals are still ***on the table****.*

TO SHOW UP

verb

ON THE TABLE

adjective

to arrive

She didn't **show up** at work until after 11:00 am.

traditional; long-standing

*Serving turkey with cranberry sauce at Thanksgiving is a **time-honored** custom in the United States.*

TO SHOW SOMEONE **UP**

verb

TIME-HONORED

adjective

to embarrass or outperform (someone)

*He **showed up** the team captain by making the most goals in last night's game.*

doing everything necessary to accomplish (something); in control of

I offered her help with the decorations for the dance, but she said she was ***on top of*** *it.*

TO SPLIT HAIRS

verb

ON TOP OF A TASK

adjective

to make small, unimportant distinctions

*They still haven't agreed on the final wording of the contract, but they **are** just **splitting hairs** now; all of the important issues have been decided.*

completely under the control of; powerless against; totally dependent upon

*Medieval peasants were often **at the mercy of** their local overlord.*

*The small ship was **at the mercy of** the storm.*

TO GO WITHOUT SAYING

verb

AT THE MERCY OF A FEW POWERFUL PEOPLE

adjective

Verb

to be obvious or self-evident

*It **goes without saying** that you should wear respectful clothes to a job interview.*

in accordance with; consistent with

*The themes of her most recent novel are **in line with** her previous work.*

TO TAKE SOMETHING **IN STRIDE**

verb

IN LINE WITH REGULATIONS

adjective

*The players **took** the insults of the opposing team **in stride** and focused on winning the game.*

to deal with (something difficult) in a calm way so that it does not cause disruptions being planned or produced; in process

*A sequel to that movie is **in the works**.*

TO WIPE SOMETHING **OUT**

verb

IN THE WORKS

adjective

to destroy (something) completely

*Three years of drought **wiped out** the region's agriculture.*

ready to act or be used at any time

Newspaper columnists often keep one idea ***in the wings*** *in case of writer's block.*

There were many people waiting ***in the wings*** *to take over when she retired.*

[a reference to the *wings* of a theater, where actors wait to go on stage]

TO SAVE ONE'S BREATH

verb

IN THE WINGS

adjective

Pronoun

to refrain from saying something that is useless or unnecessary

She won't stop smoking no matter what you say; ***save your breath.***

particularly valuable; especially in demand

In today's job market, computer skills are ***at a premium****.*

TO SAVE FACE

verb

AT A PREMIUM

adjective

to preserve one's dignity or honor; to avoid embarrassment

*He **saved face** by resigning from his job before he could be fired.*

in contact with; in communication with

We used to be close friends, but I haven't been ***in touch with*** *him for several years now.*

I really hope that I will keep ***in touch with*** *my college roommates after we graduate.*

TO FILL OUT A FORM

verb

IN TOUCH WITH SOMEONE

adjective

to complete (a form)

*He **has filled out** all of his college applications.*

in complete agreement

They had some arguments about the renovation in the beginning, but now they are ***on the same page****.*

verb

TO BIDE ONE'S TIME

ON THE SAME PAGE

adjective

Pronoun

to wait patiently

She's living with her parents for a while, ***biding her time*** *until she finds the right apartment.*

on the way; being developed

She published two books last year, and she already has another one ***in the pipeline****.*

TO KEEP HER **ON** HER **TOES**

verb

IN THE PIPELINE

adjective

to force (someone) to stay alert

*Our teacher **keeps** us **on** our **toes** by asking questions throughout his lectures.*

ready for or able to do something

*It is a very steep mountain; are you sure you're **up to** the hike?*

TO KEEP TRACK OF

verb

FEELING **UP TO** IT

adjective

Pronoun

to keep a record of; to stay informed about

*She **kept track of** her expenses so that she could be reimbursed.*

relaxed; laid-back; restrained

We are having a party, but it won't be anything big, just a ***low-key*** *gathering of friends.*

Idiom

TO SLIP SOMEONE'S **MIND**

verb

LOW-KEY

adjective

to be forgotten by someone

I was supposed to buy milk on the way home, but it completely ***slipped my mind.***

scarce; insufficiently available; running out

*We have plenty of food left, but water is **in short supply**.*

Idiom

TO PAVE THE WAY

verb

IN SHORT SUPPLY

adjective

to make future accomplishments possible; to prepare the way

The achievements of pioneering female scientists like Marie Curie ***paved the way*** *for later generations of women in science.*

[*Way* is an old-fashioned word for road; *paving* a road makes it easier and faster to travel on.]

unresolved; not yet settled

We are going to go on vacation this summer, but we haven't decided where yet; our plans are still ***up in the air***.

TO TAKE IT EASY

verb

UP IN THE AIR

adjective

to relax; to be idle

Last summer I worked 40 hours a week, but this year I ***am taking it easy.***

preoccupied with; completely absorbed in

*He was so **wrapped up in** the baseball game on television that he didn't hear me walk in.*

THAT NAME IS STARTING **TO RING A BELL**

verb

to bring back a memory; to sound familiar

I don't recognize her face, but her voice ***rings a bell.***

Pronoun

WRAPPED UP IN SOMETHING

adjective

used as an abbreviation or shortened form of

Did you know that the word 'pram' is ***short for*** *'perambulator'?*

Idiom

TO PUT THE RUMORS **TO REST**

verb

‘FYI’ IS **SHORT FOR** ‘FOR YOUR INFORMATION.’

adjective

to put a stop to; to end; to quell

If you are afraid of flying, the new technology in these planes should ***put*** *your fears* ***to rest.***

in the act of committing a crime

*They caught the thief **red-handed** with the stolen jewelry in his pockets.*

TO PIN DOWN THE DETAILS

verb

RED-HANDED

adjective

to define firmly; to figure out

The wedding is supposed to be this summer, but they haven't ***pinned down*** *the date yet.*

coming up in the future

*We aren't very busy at the moment, but we have some major projects **on the horizon**.*

idiom

TO FIELD QUESTIONS

verb

ON THE HORIZON

adjective

Noun

to answer questions from a group of people

After his speech, he ***fielded questions*** *from the audience.*

undecided; unable to make up one's mind

*He is still **on the fence** about which candidate to vote for.*

Idiom

verb

TO COUNT AS

ON THE FENCE

adjective

to be considered; to qualify as

Astronomy 101 ***counts as*** *a science course for the school's distribution requirement.*

following a course that is likely to fail

*He hasn't been making progress with his research and seems to be **on the wrong track**.*

See ***on the right track***.

TO COUNT ON

verb

ON THE WRONG TRACK

adjective

to rely on; to depend on

We need to be home early because Mom ***is counting on*** *us to help her with dinner.*

following a course that is likely to be successful

I don't know the answer yet, but I think I am ***on the right track****.*

See ***on the wrong track***.

TO KEEP A THREAT **AT BAY**

verb

ON THE RIGHT TRACK

adjective

to make (something) stay away; to ward off

*I **have been keeping** the flu **at bay** by resting and drinking lots of orange juice.*

*The moat around the castle was designed to **hold** invaders **at bay**.*

responsible for; in control of

*You will be **in charge of** refreshments for our next meeting.*

TO FIGURE OUT

verb

IN CHARGE OF

adjective

to determine or conclude

*The mechanic **figured out** that the problems were being caused by a leak in my car's fuel line.*

denoting a situation in which both parties benefit

> *He will get professional experience, and you will get a web page at a discount: it's a* ***win-win*** *arrangement.*

Also (informally) as a noun: *it was a* ***win-win***.

TO CUT BACK ON LONG-DISTANCE PHONE CALLS

verb

A **WIN-WIN** SITUATION

adjective

to use or do less of (something)

His doctor told him that he should ***cut back on*** *sugar.*

having no possibility of a positive outcome

*It was a **no-win** situation: we either had to pay the fine or pay a lawyer to fight it.*

See ***win-win***.

Adjective

TO CUT OFF

verb

A **NO-WIN** PREDICAMENT

adjective

1. to interrupt; 2. to stop or discontinue

*She rudely **cut** him **off** in the middle of his story.*

*The storm **cut off** the city's supply of electricity.*

complete; mature; fully developed

Her hobby of baking cookies has become a ***full-fledged*** *business, with stores all over the city.*

TO CUT TO THE CHASE

verb

FULL-FLEDGED

adjective

to get directly to the point

He started describing all of the different features, but we were in a hurry, so we asked him to ***cut to the chase.***

extremely agitated or upset; distraught

*He came home three hours late, and his mother was **beside herself** with worry.*

TO COME AROUND

verb

BESIDE ONESELF

adjective

Noun

to eventually agree to something

My father doesn't like the idea of me going to college so far away from home, but I'm sure he'll ***come around.***

under control

Now that our rent is higher, we will have to keep our spending ***in check****.*

TO COME DOWN TO

verb

IN CHECK

adjective

to have as an essential point; to be dependent upon

There are all sorts of fad diets around, but healthy weight loss ***comes down to*** *two factors: eating well and exercising regularly.*

very poor; destitute

*A decade ago he was a **down-and-out** alcoholic, but today he owns his own business and has been sober for 8 years.*

TO COME ALONG

verb

1. to accompany; 2. to progress

He invited a friend ***to come along.***

There were a lot of construction problems at first, but the new house ***is*** *finally* ***coming along.***

DOWN AND OUT

adjective

reasonable and practical; realistic

She seems remarkably ***down to earth*** *for the daughter of a wealthy celebrity.*

TO BEAR FRUIT

verb

DOWN TO EARTH

adjective

to produce results; to be successful

After twenty years of research, our effort to cure the disease ***is*** *finally* ***bearing fruit.***

unimportant or irrelevant

*We accept anyone who can play chess; your age is **neither here nor there**.*

TO TAKE ITS TOLL

verb

NEITHER HERE NOR THERE

adjective

to have a negative effect

*The drought **took its toll** on the crops, and the harvest was much smaller than usual.*

*She looks exhausted. All of those late nights of studying **are** finally **taking their toll.***

unable to think of anything to say; speechless

When they told her father they were getting married, he was ***at a loss for words****.*

TO PUT OFF A MEETING

verb

AT A LOSS FOR WORDS

adjective

to postpone

*Our teacher **put** the test **off** until next week.*

directly related to the topic at hand; relevant

*The testimony of the star witness in the case was concise and **to the point**.*

See ***beside the point***.

TO PASS UP AN OPPORTUNITY

verb

to decline; to fail to take advantage of

She ***passed up*** *a scholarship at a prestigious university because the school didn't have a good soccer team.*

adjective

TO THE POINT

irrelevant; unimportant

The real issue in the renovation is that we need more space; the color of the carpet is ***beside the point****.*

See ***to the point***.

TO PUT ONE'S FINGER ON A PIECE OF INFORMATION

verb

BESIDE THE POINT

adjective

to identify; to pinpoint

There must be something missing, but I can't ***put my finger on*** *what it is.*

on the verge of being recalled

I can't quite remember his name, but it's ***on the tip of my tongue****.*

TO TURN A BLIND EYE TO A PROBLEM

verb

ON THE TIP OF ONE'S TONGUE

adjective

to ignore; to overlook

*The superintendent accused local schools of **turning a blind eye** to plagiarism and cheating.*

unexceptional; ordinary

Despite all of the attention he has gotten in the press, I think he is really just a ***run-of-the-mill*** *portrait painter.*

TO TAKE NOTE OF THE CHANGES

verb

RUN OF THE MILL

adjective

to notice; to observe

He didn't immediately ***take note of*** *her new haircut.*

denoting administrative or clerical work that does not involve physical labor

*The Internet boom has created a lot of office jobs for **white-collar** workers.*

See ***blue collar***.

Adverb

TO FALL INTO PLACE

verb

WHITE COLLAR

adjective

to turn out as hoped for

We were afraid that we would never finish planning our wedding, but everything seems ***to be falling into place.***

involving or denoting physical labor

*During the summer, he does **blue-collar** jobs like construction work and house painting.*

See ***white collar***.

TO FALL OUT WITH SOMEONE

verb

BLUE COLLAR

adjective

to have a serious disagreement

*They **fell out with** each other years ago over who would run the family business.*

Also as a noun: *to have a **falling-out** with someone.*

conducted lawfully and openly; legitimate; honest

*The deal sounded suspicious, but my lawyer assured me that it was completely **above board**.*

See ***under the table***.

TO FALL SHORT

verb

ABOVE BOARD

adjective

to fail to meet expectations

*Our profits for last year **fell short.***

steady and balanced; moving calmly forward

The local economy went through some difficult times when the factory closed, but it has been ***on an even keel*** *for many years.*

Also even-keeled: *She has an* ***even-keeled*** *personality.*

[A *keel* is a structure on the bottom of a boat that keeps it stable.]

TO MUDDLE THROUGH

verb

ON AN EVEN KEEL

adjective

to find a way despite difficulty or disorganization; to manage

I didn't know anything about how to direct a play, but I ***muddled through.***

unprepared

She did well for most of the interview, but she was caught ***off guard*** *by the last question.*

TO BRING SOMEONE **UP TO DATE**

verb

OFF GUARD

adjective

to give (someone) the latest information

*Since you have been absent, talk to me after class, and I will **bring** you **up to date**.*

competent at one's profession

Any coach ***worth his salt*** *would have taught you how to stretch your muscles after practice.*

Adverb

TO PUT A PROJECT **ON HOLD**

verb

WORTH ONE'S SALT

adjective

to stop (something) temporarily; to suspend

*We **are putting** the renovation **on hold** until next summer.*

to be skeptical about (something)

Since he has strong views on this subject, I ***took*** *his report* ***with a grain of salt****.*

Adverb

TO RULE OUT A POSSIBILITY

verb

TO TAKE SOMETHING **WITH A GRAIN OF SALT**

verb

to exclude (something) as a possible option or explanation

*We haven't decided where to spend our honeymoon yet, but we have **ruled out** going on a cruise.*

*The doctor told her that tests had **ruled out** cancer as the cause of her symptoms.*

to give (something) up

*Even when he went to college, he refused **to part with** his teddy bear.*

TO PLAY DOWN AN ACHIEVEMENT

verb

TO PART WITH A POSSESSION

verb

to minimize the importance of

The other students were impressed by her famous father, but she always ***played down*** *her glamorous background.*

The opposite is to *play up*: 'to exaggerate.'

to try; to make an attempt

*I've never baked a pie before, but I **am taking a stab at** it this weekend.*

*They asked him **to make a stab at** creating a web page.*

TO PLAY IT SAFE

verb

TO TAKE A STAB AT DOING SOMETHING

verb

to avoid taking risks

*They **played it safe** and allowed two hours for the drive to the airport.*

to bear the consequences of a mistake or misdeed

*The school principal made the whole class **pay the price** for graffiti made by one student.*

TO PLAY WITH FIRE

verb

TO PAY THE PRICE FOR A CRIME

verb

to do something dangerous or risky

We warned the diplomat that he ***was playing with fire*** *by getting involved in local politics.*

to decide; to make a decision

*He got into three different colleges, so now he is trying **to make up his mind** about which one to attend.*

TO KEEP SOMETHING **IN MIND**

verb

TO MAKE UP ONE'S MIND

verb

to remember and account for (something)

*While writing your essay, **keep in mind** that you will get a higher grade if it has a clear argument.*

to do things in the wrong order

Critics say that buying furniture for the new library before the architect has been chosen ***is putting the cart before the horse****.*

Noun

TO BARGAIN FOR

verb

TO PUT THE CART BEFORE THE HORSE

verb

to expect or be prepared for

The vacationers got more rain than they ***had bargained for*** *when monsoon season hit a few weeks early.*

to convince (someone) to do something

*He didn't want to join the team, but they **talked** him **into** it.*

Noun

TO DEAL WITH A PROBLEM

verb

TO TALK SOMEONE **INTO** DOING SOMETHING

verb

to handle or control

*They are finding new ways of **dealing with** the rising cost of college tuition.*

to align oneself with one of the sides in a dispute

*Parents should avoid **taking sides** when their children argue.*

TO TAKE OVER THE COMPANY

verb

Noun

TO TAKE SIDES

verb

to take control of

He is difficult to work because he usually tries ***to take over*** *the most interesting projects.*

to participate

*Fifty nations **took part** in the conference at which the Charter of the United Nations was drafted in 1945.*

TO RUN OUT OF PROVISIONS

verb

TO TAKE PART

verb

to use up (a supply of something)

I couldn't make cookies because I **ran out of** sugar.

to endure or tolerate

Rather than disciplining students who are late for class, she ***puts up with*** *their behavior.*

TO TAKE ON SOMEONE OR SOMETHING

verb

TO PUT UP WITH SOMETHING UNPLEASANT

verb

1. to hire (an employee); 2. to confront; to fight against

*They decided **to take** him **on** as a research assistant.*

*The environmental group **is taking on** a big corporation it accuses of polluting the lake.*

to settle down; to establish a permanent residence

*After years of traveling, he is finally **putting down roots** by buying a house in his hometown.*

TO BEAT AROUND THE BUSH

verb

TO PUT DOWN ROOTS

verb

to avoid talking directly about something

The community meeting was frustrating because the mayor kept ***beating around the bush*** *instead of addressing the important issues facing our community.*

Test Preparation

From the creators of the #1 TOEFL® Exam Course

TOEFL Idioms Flashcards is an indispensable study tool for TOEFL test takers and others learning English. Idioms can be difficult to learn in any language, but they are especially challenging in English.

- **350 idioms to help you pass the TOEFL exam**
- **Definitions plus sample sentences in context**
- **Portable and easy-to-use for learning English**
- **Clarification of especially difficult idioms**
- **Convenient, portable format to take with you anywhere**

US: $12.00 CAN: $15.00

ISBN-13: 978-1-4195-9148-8
ISBN-10: 1-4195-9148-7
51200
9 781419 591488

COMPILED BY KATHERINE MARTIN

Cover design by Carly Schnur

10061200 KAPLAN Published by Kaplan Publishing